MACHINES ON THE MOVE

TRACTORS

by Natalie Deniston

TABLE OF CONTENTS

Tadpole Books, an imprint of Jump! Library by FlutterBee

WORDS TO KNOW

cab

farm

lifts

pulls

pushes

tires

TRACTORS

Look! A tractor.

tire

It has big tires.

cab

It has a cab.

It lifts.

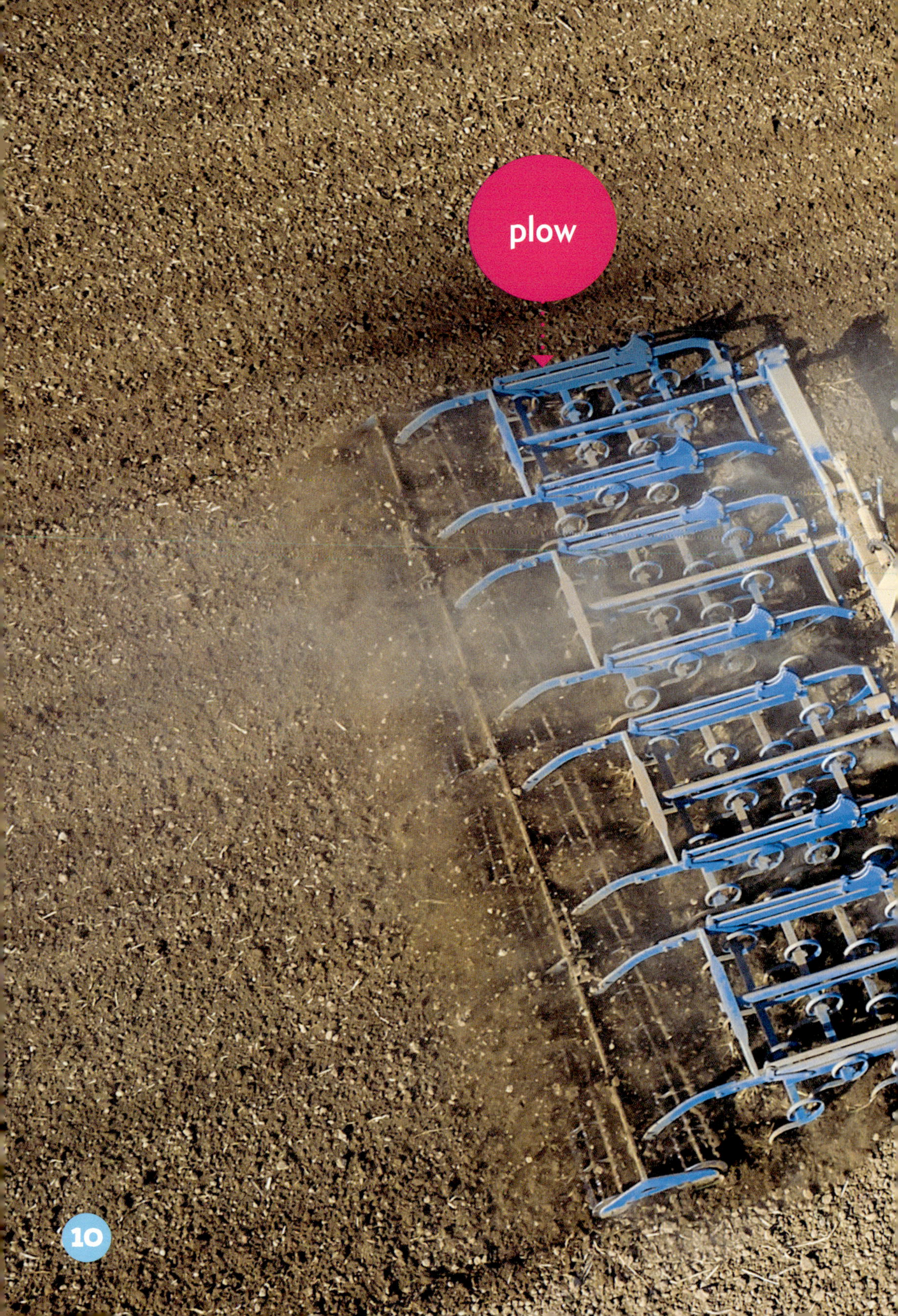
plow

It pulls.

snow

It pushes.

It helps on the farm.

LET'S REVIEW!

Tractors do many jobs on a farm. What is this one doing?

INDEX